THE GIFT

Mildred Inez Lewis

BROADWAY PLAY PUBLISHING INC
New York
www.broadwayplaypublishing.com
info@broadwayplaypublishing.com

THE GIFT

First edition: May 2021
I S B N: 978-0-88145-901-2

Book design: Marie Donovan
Page make-up: Adobe InDesign
Typeface: Palatino

CHARACTERS & SETTING

SUSANNAH HAWKINS, *19, white, the wife of Enoch and widow of James Tilden. She is a Beasley, one of South Carolina's first families. Land rich and cash poor. No wilting southern belle, she is a sturdy woman.*

ENOCH ROBERT "BOBBY" HAWKINS, *24, white,* SUSANNAH'*s husband, and a New Jersey transplant. He is a patrician and a bit of a dandy.*

Time: 1850s

Place: a South Carolina rice plantation

PRODUCTION NOTE

The play may be performed with or without an intermission. If one is desired, it should be between Scenes 6 and 7.

Scene 1

(Saturday afternoon. Spring)

*(*SUSANNAH *runs in carrying her wedding veil.)*

(Her husband BOBBY *follows. A city boy, he's winded.* SUSANNAH *puts on the veil and twirls.)*

SUSANNAH: Catch me.

BOBBY: I don't think I can.

SUSANNAH: *(Laughing)* I thought you Yankees were supposed to be quick.

*(*BOBBY *chases* SUSANNAH*. She's too fast for him. He raises his hands in surrender.)*

BOBBY: Uncle.

SUSANNAH: I win.

BOBBY: Yes ma'am, you do.

SUSANNAH: Go again?

*(*SUSANNAH *starts to run again.* BOBBY *points to the veil.)*

BOBBY: I don't think you should wear that inside the house.

SUSANNAH: Why not?

BOBBY: I mean it.

SUSANNAH: Come for it then.

BOBBY: You should take it off.

SUSANNAH: So very serious. Sometimes you border on the dour, Mr Hawkins. Planting's gone well. I want to celebrate.

BOBBY: It's bad luck.

SUSANNAH: It's bad luck for the groom to see the dress before the wedding. Not after.

(BOBBY *crosses his arms.)*

SUSANNAH: Whatever's the matter?

BOBBY: We shouldn't risk anything that keeps you from conceiving.

SUSANNAH: That's what you're worried about?

BOBBY: It's been nearly four months and there's still no sign.

(SUSANNAH *quickly takes off the veil.)*

BOBBY: My aunt told me things before our nuptials. If a lady handles the articles from her wedding before her time comes, it can close her womb.

SUSANNAH: Like the evil eye?

BOBBY: I guess.

SUSANNAH: *(Alarmed)* I've been taking my wedding dress out nearly every day.

BOBBY: Why?

SUSANNAH: I like the touch of it against my skin.

BOBBY: I've never seen you do this.

SUSANNAH: I've been hiding it from you. I didn't want to seem like a frivolous southern belle.

BOBBY: It's all right. But you best stop.

SUSANNAH: Yes, sir.

(SUSANNAH *salutes* BOBBY *playfully.)*

BOBBY: No more secrets between us.

SUSANNAH: Oh, I don't know about that. Everybody knows you can't tell husbands everything. We ladies need to keep certain things strictly to ourselves.

BOBBY: I'm a northern man. I'll want a touch more frankness. Especially in this situation.

SUSANNAH: Do you really think it's why I haven't conceived?

BOBBY: We shouldn't take chances.

SUSANNAH: It took my mother nearly two years to have her first.

BOBBY: Your big brother George?

SUSANNAH: No, the first boy's name was Moses.

BOBBY: You've never mentioned him.

SUSANNAH: He was stillborn.

BOBBY: My mother lost two.

SUSANNAH: My parents buried three, then Beatrice took my mother with her.

(BOBBY *takes* SUSANNAH*'s hands in his.)*

SUSANNAH: Daddy said they were too sweet for this world, so the good lord called them home.

BOBBY: That's exactly right. It's probably what drew us together.

SUSANNAH: What's that?

BOBBY: We're two motherless children with only one father left between us. And you a widow. That's why it's important that we bring forth new life.

SUSANNAH: Maybe I'll be slow like my mother. I hope that's it.

BOBBY: With respect, your mother hadn't been used before her marriage.

SUSANNAH: Wilbur and I had hardly been together when the 'fluenza took him.

BOBBY: I don't mean it in a bad way. It might have something to do with it is all.

SUSANNAH: Do you ever regret—?

BOBBY: Never. You're the one for me.

SUSANNAH: Would you have felt differently, if I had had children?

BOBBY: That definitely would not have changed my mind. It would've proved you were fertile.

*(*BOBBY *laughs, notices* SUSANNAH*'s discomfort, then puts his arms around her.)*

BOBBY: Which I am confident you are.

SUSANNAH: You're a good man, Enoch Robert Hawkins.

BOBBY: A man's not a man until he has children and a wife. I've been a success all my life. I don't intend to begin failing now.

*(*SUSANNAH *gives* BOBBY *the veil.)*

SUSANNAH: I've sometimes sensed that people might be whispering.

BOBBY: They've said as much to me directly.

SUSANNAH: You never said a word.

BOBBY: A gentleman doesn't complain.

SUSANNAH: What you must think of us.

BOBBY: I expected it. People always blame the outsider.

SUSANNAH: Those old maids are just jealous. You don't listen to a word they say.

BOBBY: I wouldn't if it were just them.

SUSANNAH: My brothers?

*(*BOBBY *nods.)*

SUSANNAH: I wish Mee Maw was still living. She knew how to keep them in line.

BOBBY: I know it's not the same, but you have me now.

*(*SUSANNAH *cups* BOBBY*'s face.)*

SUSANNAH: Beloved.

*(*BOBBY *and* SUSANNAH *kiss.)*

BOBBY: *(Jokingly)* I think we both have work to do. Shall we?

*(*BOBBY *sits to review the farm's ledgers.* SUSANNAH *takes up her sewing. They work together silently for a moment.)*

SUSANNAH: Bobby?

BOBBY: Yes, darling?

SUSANNAH: I've wondering…

BOBBY: About?

SUSANNAH: About the rest of the dowry. My family paid for our planting seed. They want to be paid back.

BOBBY: We weren't married when that seed was purchased.

SUSANNAH: We were betrothed. My family considers it your responsibility.

BOBBY: Is that the law here?

SUSANNAH: Not the literal law, but a Beasley tradition. My father's been inquiring. And my brothers.

BOBBY: About such a trivial amount?

SUSANNAH: You know how they go on. It would mean a great deal to me if you would pay them.

BOBBY: Are your brothers in financial difficulty?

SUSANNAH: No. Not exactly.

BOBBY: With the amount I've already settled on you…

SUSANNAH: I know. You've been more generous than any widow could reasonably expect.

BOBBY: It was important to me that everyone know my wife is highly valued. You're a reflection of me and part of the Hawkins lineage.

SUSANNAH: What about my kin?

BOBBY: The illustrious Beasleys are included in that sentiment.

SUSANNAH: You don't know everything you should about us. For all our storied history, we've been having struggles. These last few growing seasons have been very hard. This year's been especially bad.

BOBBY: The Panic.

SUSANNAH: Daddy's had to borrow.

BOBBY: That's not fiscally sound.

SUSANNAH: It was the only way. This town depends upon us to keep up appearances. We set the tone.

BOBBY: If money's a problem, belts have to be tightened. I've noticed your father has a number of workers with seemingly little to do.

SUSANNAH: They're elderly or infirm. We have an obligation.

BOBBY: They may need to be turned out.

SUSANNAH: Is this how people up north think? These people aren't workers, they're family.

BOBBY: That's an imprudent way to think.

SUSANNAH: Some things are more important than money. Everything can't be reduced to a transaction.

BOBBY: If your family needs financial support from me, maybe they could consider training some of the slaves to take their place. Gradually.

SUSANNAH: They could never. They haven't got the capacity. If you're not in a position to help, or it goes against your philosophy.

BOBBY: It's a lot to take in. I only wish you'd said something earlier.

SUSANNAH: You can understand my hesitation. I didn't marry you for your money. I have land.

BOBBY: Of course I'll help.

*(*SUSANNAH *breathes a huge sigh of relief.* BOBBY *laughs reassuringly.)*

BOBBY: What a pair we make. I don't know how many times I have to reassure you. Nothing can turn me against you.

SUSANNAH: You speak with such conviction. I admire it so.

BOBBY: I'm speaking from the heart.

SUSANNAH: Yet, couples can grow apart over matters like this.
(She raises one hand and puts the other across her heart.)
I promise never to give you a reason to wish yourself back on the other side of the Mason Dixie. I'll let my family know in no uncertain terms, this is the last time.

BOBBY: Your brothers. Oh my.

SUSANNAH: It's something to be raised the only girl among boys. Sisters seem to live in their own little world. Their men folk well meaning, distant protectors. But when it's one girl alone? They'd spoil me one minute, roughhouse me the next. Once mama was gone, it seemed like there was no tenderness left in them. When Mee Maw passed, they turned wild.

BOBBY: We'll bring them in line.

SUSANNAH: How soon do you think—?

BOBBY: I could retrieve the necessary funds myself. It would mean a trip back to New Jersey—

SUSANNAH: No, sir. That could take weeks. I refuse to let you out of my sight for that long. My brothers can wait for the stagecoach to arrive.
(She kisses her thanks.)

BOBBY: Want to see a secret? Take your mind off this business?

SUSANNAH: I would.

*(*BOBBY *takes a fine calf skin pouch from his pocket. He dangles it. It holds a male slave's now desiccated middle finger tip.)*

SUSANNAH: What is it?

*(*BOBBY *opens the pouch.)*

BOBBY: Look inside.

*(*SUSANNAH *does.)*

SUSANNAH: Ooo!

BOBBY: Something isn't it?

SUSANNAH: The skin's gray and shiny. Can I hold it?

BOBBY: No. I found it among my uncle's things the day I met you. It's my good luck charm now.

SUSANNAH: Please?

*(*SUSANNAH *puts her arms around* BOBBY*'s waist.)*

BOBBY: Would you like to retire early, Missus Hawkins?

SUSANNAH: I would.

BOBBY: Come.

*(*BOBBY *uses it to lead* SUSANNAH *into the bedroom.)*

(End scene)

Scene 2

(Evening. The sound of a retreating horse carriage)

(Lights rise as BOBBY *and* SUSANNAH *return from a formal ball.)*

(They dance to the memory of the last song they heard. They stop when they're out of breath.)

SUSANNAH: Now this was a fine evening.

BOBBY: It was indeed.

SUSANNAH: You just encountered the South Carolina version of the Virginia reel. Ours is better.

BOBBY: Says you?

SUSANNAH: Says anyone who's had the honor of trying both.

BOBBY: That fiddler was a man possessed.

SUSANNAH: My favorite's the banjo player. He sure can pick.

BOBBY: Was the older gentleman playing with spoons?

SUSANNAH: Yes, he was. That's big down here.

BOBBY: I want to try.
(He grabs two spoons from the table and attempts to play.)
If music be the food of love…

SUSANNAH: You're terrible.

BOBBY: Doesn't matter if this is our night.

*(*BOBBY *kisses* SUSANNAH *a little roughly.)*

SUSANNAH: We don't have to rush, do we? If we take our time, it's more likely to take.

BOBBY: I'm falling in love with this place. There's a graciousness here.

SUSANNAH: I haven't traveled, but I don't believe any place on earth is better. Maybe as good, but not better.

BOBBY: Some of your folks though.

SUSANNAH: You leave my people be. Besides, you seem to be getting on pretty well. I noticed you talking to Dan Henry and James.

BOBBY: Very agreeable company.

SUSANNAH: I guess they can be.

BOBBY: We shared a pint.

SUSANNAH: Or two or three.

BOBBY: I feel we're going to be great friends. I think we even favor each other.

SUSANNAH: I don't hardly think so. Dan Henry's the only red head in the county and that beanpole James has the worst cowlick in town.

BOBBY: I'll have you know James is considering a run for sheriff.

SUSANNAH: Is he now?

BOBBY: I think he could be the right man for the job.

SUSANNAH: It's not his time.

BOBBY: Are there rules about that too?

SUSANNAH: No, but there's protocol and tradition.

BOBBY: Aah.

SUSANNAH: Not to mention respecting your elders. James has never been willing to wait his turn.

BOBBY: That's not always wrong. Sometimes it's the only way things can get done.

SUSANNAH: This is why people think Yanks are pushy.

BOBBY: What do you think?

SUSANNAH: I like it. That said, you may want to keep your distance. Lots of folks here think Dan Henry and James are trouble.

BOBBY: I didn't get that impression.

SUSANNAH: We southerners are masters of feeding people with a long-handled spoon. Done right Dan Henry, your favorite red head, and James might suspect something was wrong. They'd never be able to prove it by anything was said or done.

BOBBY: I respect men willing to speak their own mind. That's the standard my daddy set for me.

SUSANNAH: I think that might work better in New Jersey than here.

BOBBY: I may want to dabble in politics myself. Not now, of course. Sometime in the future.

*(*BOBBY *rubs* SUSANNAH*'s belly.)*

SUSANNAH: Sometime in the very distant future, I hope.

BOBBY: I haven't put a timetable to it.

SUSANNAH: My family prefers to keep to itself.

BOBBY: That promotes secrets and secrets can be dangerous.

SUSANNAH: To whom?

BOBBY: Just an observation.

SUSANNAH: Truth is, all politicians are good for is meddling. We should live free like the people in the western stories. That's the way to live.

BOBBY: So you do read?

SUSANNAH: From time to time.

BOBBY: I must say, I'm relieved.

SUSANNAH: You should try them. They're much more enjoyable than those dry tomes you seem to like so much. Honestly, sometimes I worry your brain's going to explode.

*(*BOBBY *laughs.)*

BOBBY: Well, it's a shame your family feels that way. Your brothers could make a real difference on the council.

SUSANNAH: If everyone looked after their own, there wouldn't be any need for politicking.

BOBBY: We need government.

SUSANNAH: We'll have to agree to disagree. Did you all discuss anything else besides barley, hops and politics?

BOBBY: I don't think so. Why do you ask?

SUSANNAH: They've been known to complain about the way we conduct business. We don't treat the hands right. Honestly, they go on and on. You have to wonder if there is any subject about which they don't have an expert opinion.

BOBBY: Dan Henry made what I thought was a very fair point. At some point, the peculiar institution may have to be reformed.

SUSANNAH: That would devastate us. And them.

BOBBY: You don't even know what he's proposing. Hell—heck—he doesn't know himself. He wants to see improvements made, that's all.

SUSANNAH: Things are fine as they are.

BOBBY: Everything can be made better.

SUSANNAH: People shouldn't try to fix what's not broke. He and James are going to fool around and find themselves in bed with god knows who.

BOBBY: Neither one said anything disrespectful.

SUSANNAH: Or treasonous?

BOBBY: Of course not. Certainly not I.

SUSANNAH: I'm glad to hear that. Folks from up north always seem so quick to judge us.

BOBBY: Once I got here, I saw how things had to be. We don't have these big farms back home. Until you see them, you don't understand the full force of the need.

SUSANNAH: You just be careful around those two.

BOBBY: Yes, wife.

(BOBBY's dog howls.)

BOBBY: That hound is a stain on civilization. I should've left him behind in Woodbridge.

SUSANNAH: Go see what's wrong.

BOBBY: It's turned chilly. I'll light the fire when I get back.

SUSANNAH: Don't you worry. I'll do it. I'm not helpless.

BOBBY: That's the charm of a southern girl, satin over steel. When I come back, we'll get to work on making that young'un.

SUSANNAH: I'm a little bit tired after all this.

(BOBBY undoes SUSANNAH's top.)

BOBBY: I'll be right back.
(He exits.)

Scene 3

(Lunchtime, months later. SUSANNAH clears the table. BOBBY reads the paper to avoid her.)

SUSANNAH: Did you like the stew? I think it can use a touch more salt. I'll talk to mammy.

BOBBY: Salt's easier to add than take away.

SUSANNAH: Are you avoiding the question?

BOBBY: Good as always.

SUSANNAH: It looks like all you did was push the food around your plate.

BOBBY: Spoken like a frustrated mama bear.

SUSANNAH: I don't mean to nag.

BOBBY: I'm a grown man. I know to eat when I'm hungry.

SUSANNAH: I had manny make enough to last a few days.

BOBBY: It's just the two of us. We don't need that much food. Things that persist too long spoil.

(SUSANNAH *packs a lunch pail.)*

SUSANNAH: Forgive me. I must have misunderstood. I thought Brunswick stew was your favorite.

BOBBY: I enjoy it.

SUSANNAH: You prefer things not be fried. If we don't make stew, I'm not sure what else—

BOBBY: Really, it's fine. Burgoo is fine. Hoppin' John's fine. It's all fine.

SUSANNAH: It doesn't sound like it's all right to you.

BOBBY: I'll feel better when there's more than two of us rattling around this big house. A place like this should be filled with noise.

(BOBBY *gives* SUSANNAH *a goodbye peck.)*

SUSANNAH: You have much left to do?

BOBBY: No matter how hard I work, there's always something pressing left to do. It's a far cry from running a factory.

(BOBBY *stands. A leather African style necklace with a totem made from hair drops from his lap.* SUSANNAH *grabs it.)*

SUSANNAH: What's this thing?

BOBBY: I found it.

SUSANNAH: Where?

BOBBY: In the cotton fields.

SUSANNAH: It looks like some kind of totem. Something those females would wear. Surely, it's the enemy's work.

BOBBY: We can't be sure of that.

SUSANNAH: I won't have a graven image in our home.

BOBBY: It interests me so it stays.

*(*BOBBY *takes it from* SUSANNAH.*)*

SUSANNAH: Wherever you put it, place a cross near it. If touching a veil would curse us—

BOBBY: I hadn't thought of that. I'll keep it away from the house.
(He goes to the door.)

SUSANNAH: Don't forget to gather some alfalfa.

*(*BOBBY *groans.)*

SUSANNAH: Horse feed's running low for us and daddy.

BOBBY: Everything can't be done in a day. Since your brothers are busy, I would ask Dan Henry or James for help.

SUSANNAH: Please don't.

BOBBY: I know. They're out of favor with your clan. If I'd known how short of help the farm was, despite all the hangers on. I wish someone had thought to mention that before our wedding.

SUSANNAH: You like all those fancy sayings, let the buyer beware.

BOBBY: That applies to dry goods, not man power.

SUSANNAH: You can't say daddy didn't give you the grand tour.

BOBBY: He did. I guess it was up to me to read between the lines.

(BOBBY's dog barks. SUSANNAH hands him the lunch pail.)

SUSANNAH: Maybe your hound—

BOBBY: I don't want her getting used to table scraps.

SUSANNAH: Surely one time wouldn't hurt.

BOBBY: She'd grow to expect it.

SUSANNAH: Seems there's nothing I can do to satisfy you today. Maybe we should read some scripture when you return.

BOBBY: Children do that with parents. Every one stands alone before the creator. Study to show yourself approved.
(He exits without his lunch.)

(SUSANNAH goes to the Bible stand, kneels and touches her womb.)

SUSANNAH: *(Whispers)* Please.

(End scene)

Scene 4

(An afternoon a few days later. SUSANNAH, still not pregnant, sits across from her husband at the table. It is desperately hot and humid.)

BOBBY: It's as bad as the tropics.

SUSANNAH: You can't pay humidity any nevermind. It's just a fact of life here.

BOBBY: So I see.

SUSANNAH: If I'd moved to New Jersey, I'd never think of complaining about snow.

BOBBY: Snow doesn't leave one enervated.

SUSANNAH: Whatever that means.

BOBBY: It means—

SUSANNAH: Stop. I don't want to know. Thinking makes me perspire.

BOBBY: Where on earth do you get these notions from?

SUSANNAH: One cools down with a glass of lemonade, not a book. We can call for someone to fan.

BOBBY: I see no benefit to stirring hot air around.
(Stands)
I'm going to try lying down for a spell. I took no rest last night. Kept waking up in a swelter.

SUSANNAH: I know. I was besides you.

BOBBY: I forget.

SUSANNAH: Should I come with you?

BOBBY: Another body just makes more heat. I need to rise by dawn. I'm helping in your father's fields tomorrow.

SUSANNAH: I know you're doing all this for me.

BOBBY: I don't want your people thinking a Yank can't handle the climate.

SUSANNAH: With all this, do you still love me?

BOBBY: That's a silly question.

SUSANNAH: If feels like you're all business most of the time.

BOBBY: Until our family begins, what else is there to talk about?

SUSANNAH: I'm trying. You don't have to be so crisp in your manner toward me.

BOBBY: It's the heat. I can hardly think straight.

SUSANNAH: Other people are noticing.

BOBBY: By other people you mean your brothers, don't you? Or does that include your father as well?
(Imitates her father)
"Desperate men fan through the South, Bobby. Looking for widows to make their fortune. I will not allow my daughter to be subject to this. We'll protect her to the last." I was never a vulture coming to pick meat from your bones. In fact, things could be seen as the exact opposite.

SUSANNAH: We'll try our best to pay you back.

BOBBY: It's in the past. We need never speak of it again.

SUSANNAH: When you came, we didn't know what to think. What did we know of men from up north? You didn't work or fight for your land. It's easy to be generous with things you had no hand in earning.

*(*BOBBY *sits.)*

BOBBY: This conversation's certainly a revelation.

SUSANNAH: It's different when your own blood and sweat have watered the soil. You must know that to be true.

BOBBY: I embraced another man's woman and made her my wife. I believe that proves my good intentions.

SUSANNAH: I'm grateful—

BOBBY: As you should be. This corner of the world is littered with widows and spinsters. What are their prospects?

SUSANNAH: Dismal.

BOBBY: Not dismal. Nonexistent.

SUSANNAH: You can't deny that our properties being so close to each other helped make our match.

BOBBY: It made the match more attractive. It is true I might not've found you if my uncle hadn't passed on. But I had choices. I could simply have sold the properties and returned to New Jersey. I married for love. I'm young and strong and willing to sacrifice for a helpmeet, but not for a wife who doesn't treat me with respect.

SUSANNAH: I never—!

BOBBY: That is a humiliation I will not endure. Not with everything else I have to carry. Besides, we have other problems.

SUSANNAH: What problems?

BOBBY: Worry's not good for your constitution.

SUSANNAH: Burdens shared are burdens halved. I tried to protect you from my family's secret. When I told you, we grew stronger for it.

BOBBY: The soil's more depleted than I thought. We can't get the north field to drain. Though I'm not sure it matters. When it's dry, it collapses into dust.

SUSANNAH: My brothers have never mentioned a problem.

BOBBY: They don't seem to be able to take it in. "Our land's good. It's always been good. It will always be good."

SUSANNAH: This one time, my brothers are right. We've put everything we know into this land.

BOBBY: I'm sure they did their best. It's just not going to be enough. We have to allow the soil to lie fallow.

SUSANNAH: That would be drastic.

BOBBY: If not that, then we'll have to increase our stock. We can keep breeding and selling off until there's enough to put the whole farm back into production.

SUSANNAH: Like common traders?

BOBBY: My family is in trade.

SUSANNAH: That's different. It's the north. I don't want my family reduced to scrounging for another dollar. Life should be about finer things.

BOBBY: You'll get no argument for me on that. But our circumstances are growing serious. We're in no position to look down our noses at any viable path forward.

SUSANNAH: Surely with your resources.

BOBBY: With my parents gone, I have my sisters to think of. They'll all three need dowries.

SUSANNAH: Would people have to know?

BOBBY: I'll do things as discreetly as possible. I can't promise no one will find out.

SUSANNAH: I trust you.

BOBBY: It won't be easy, but if we're disciplined it could work. I can't see another way. I've worked out the figures.
(He displays the ledger.)

SUSANNAH: I never learned how to read those properly.

BOBBY: Then trust. If God be with us—maybe not this year—but soon the property will be on a sound footing.

SUSANNAH: Maybe you should talk this over with daddy.

BOBBY: This is our problem to solve. If you want to go back home—

SUSANNAH: I'm sorry. That was panic talking.

BOBBY: In panic, truth?

SUSANNAH: No. You're my family now.

(SUSANNAH wraps herself around BOBBY.)

(End scene)

Scene 5

*(*SUSANNAH *folds linen at the table.)*

*(*BOBBY *enters. He's exhausted, barefoot. His cuffs and pant legs almost drip blood.)*

SUSANNAH: Mercy. Where are your boots?

BOBBY: I left them outside. They were drenched in blood. I laid them on the grass.

SUSANNAH: Better move them before the dogs get after them. They'll gnaw the leather to where you won't be able to wear them again.

*(*BOBBY *exits, then quickly returns with the boots. He sits heavily.)*

BOBBY: They'll be ruined in here too. Can anything dry in this humidity?

SUSANNAH: I'll work the leather.

*(*BOBBY *falls quiet.* SUSANNAH *kneels in front of him.)*

SUSANNAH: Was it a good kill?

BOBBY: I had to stick the first ewe over and over again. I missed the vein the first time. Clumsy.

SUSANNAH: Not clumsy, inexperienced.

BOBBY: I was sweating like a hog. It streamed into my eyes and ran down inside my ears. I hoped your brothers would finish her, but I guess it was yet another test.

SUSANNAH: Did you let on?

BOBBY: I knew enough to know that would spell disaster.

SUSANNAH: They'd torment you 'til the end of time.

BOBBY: The slaughter wasn't what I expected. The sounds—

SUSANNAH: My Yankee's no longer a gentleman farmer. Baptism by blood.

BOBBY: It gave me true respect for the work. The hunt doesn't compare.

SUSANNAH: What did you think it would be?

BOBBY: Cleaner. I hope you never have to witness it.

SUSANNAH: I have. It can't be helped on a farm. There's nothing between us and birth, death.

BOBBY: The stench left my nose raw. So much blood and the steam from the innards. I couldn't look the dying thing in the face. I felt ashamed somehow.

SUSANNAH: I used to feel that way, too. When the bulls would mount the cows or Daddy was gutting fish, I always tried to look away. He wouldn't let me. He and my brothers would cackle and laugh.

BOBBY: I'm not giving up. If your brothers can manage, so can I. I'm determined to make my bride proud.

SUSANNAH: You have. Never doubt that. Let's think of more pleasant things. You never said how good the kill was. How many dead?

BOBBY: I lost count, but more than forty.

SUSANNAH: That must put us much closer to what we need.

BOBBY: We're nearly there.

SUSANNAH: Anything left to kill?

BOBBY: Two dozen or so goats.

(SUSANNAH *carefully lays out three killing knives.)*

BOBBY: What're you doing?

(SUSANNAH *touches one tip to her finger and draws blood. She sucks it clean, then takes out a whetstone.)*

SUSANNAH: Presents. Use them tomorrow. They were my grandmother's. All they need is some sharpening.

BOBBY: They're not sharp enough?

SUSANNAH: A quick kill's a mercy to man and beast.

*(*SUSANNAH *hands* BOBBY *the knives.)*

SUSANNAH: Draw it across both sides. Like that. Faster. Good.

(End scene)

Scene 6

(Dawn. Pouring down, devastating rain. The sound of the storm is fearsome. SUSANNAH *paces.)*

*(*BOBBY *enters. He's disheveled and soaked. His pants are partially undone.* SUSANNAH *rushes to him.)*

SUSANNAH: I was so worried.

BOBBY: The Randall's overflowed its banks. The fields are almost completely washed out.

SUSANNAH: The east fields—

BOBBY: All of them.

SUSANNAH: We mustn't panic.

BOBBY: I don't know how many of the animals will make it.

SUSANNAH: This happened before. Daddy was able to—

*(*BOBBY *shakes* SUSANNAH.*)*

BOBBY: There's barely anything left, do you understand? We're down to nothing.

*(*SUSANNAH *rubs* BOBBY*'s shoulders. He shrugs her off.)*

SUSANNAH: We can't lose hope.

(BOBBY *holds up his hand for quiet.)*

BOBBY: Please.

SUSANNAH: How high is the water?

BOBBY: At least six feet.

SUSANNAH: Were you able to help my brothers?

BOBBY: I was too busy trying to save us. We needed every last penny to make it through the winter. Now we don't have it.

SUSANNAH: At least we still have your funds.

BOBBY: I'm a businessman. I don't throw good money after bad.

*(*SUSANNAH *stares at* BOBBY *in shock.)*

BOBBY: In time you'll thank me. Sober management guided by Christian principles is the only way.

SUSANNAH: This isn't a business. It's our home.

BOBBY: It's an investment and has to be treated as such. I don't mean to sound unfeeling.

SUSANNAH: Is that how you think of me?

BOBBY: Of course not. Susannah, now is the not the time.

SUSANNAH: Then what? How do you propose we go on?

BOBBY: We have no choice but to keep on with the plan. Work with the stock we have.

SUSANNAH: We have to try to re-plant.

BOBBY: Any seed put in ground this drenched will rot. I don't know everything about agriculture, but I'm sure of that.

SUSANNAH: We'll find a way.

BOBBY: There is a point where optimism becomes unwelcome.

SUSANNAH: We should eat.

BOBBY: Of course I'm not hungry.

SUSANNAH: We have to keep to a routine.

BOBBY: Why? How?

SUSANNAH: The line between stability and madness is slight. Order is the only thing I've seen that can keep it in place.

BOBBY: Not this time.

*(*SUSANNAH *gets food on the table.)*

SUSANNAH: I'm helping you fight with the only tools I've been given. The ones my grandmother taught my mother and I'll teach our girls.

*(*BOBBY *grabs food.)*

SUSANNAH: *(Quietly)* We are thankful for this bounty, lord. That despite it all, you keep us far from hunger and privation. Amen.

*(*BOBBY *nods his amen.)*

BOBBY: You were right. I'm starving.

SUSANNAH: You'll need your strength to guide us through this. Whatever we have to do, I'm with you.

BOBBY: I could use another helping.

*(*SUSANNAH *obliges.)*

SUSANNAH: Where were you?

BOBBY: I think that's obvious.

SUSANNAH: Before the rains.

BOBBY: What do you mean?

SUSANNAH: I went to the barn. There was no one there.

BOBBY: We'd left.

SUSANNAH: You said you'd be there all day.

BOBBY: I didn't know I was required to make a report.

SUSANNAH: I'm not presuming—

BOBBY: After we finished in the barn, I rode to the outer buildings at approximately quarter to two.

SUSANNAH: I don't understand.

*(*BOBBY *finishes eating.)*

BOBBY: Help me get these things off.

*(*SUSANNAH *helps* BOBBY *off with his boots.)*

BOBBY: Now the pants.

*(*SUSANNAH *starts to tug at the pants.)*

BOBBY: Careful. The flesh is tender. We rode hard.

*(*SUSANNAH *works more gently.)*

BOBBY: That's it.

*(*BOBBY *is turned on.)*

SUSANNAH: I don't understand why you needed to go out that far. It's dangerous out there even without the rains. With them, you could've been cut off.

BOBBY: I was at the quarters.

*(*SUSANNAH *stops undressing* BOBBY.*)*

SUSANNAH: Why? Only the overseer needs to go there.

BOBBY: Finish.

SUSANNAH: I—

BOBBY: I wouldn't ask if I didn't need your help. My fingers are stiff.

*(*SUSANNAH *resumes helping him undress.)*

BOBBY: The chickens were already down with fever. Now this. It's like the plagues of Egypt. One disaster after another. If I weren't a believing man, I'd say we were cursed.

SUSANNAH: Surely the overseer and his drivers know what to do at the quarters without your help.

BOBBY: I'd been there before.

SUSANNAH: I don't understand.

BOBBY: We need ready cash, so I've been taking action.

(SUSANNAH realizes that BOBBY has been trying to impregnate the slaves.)

SUSANNAH: Even if you managed to… The money would be nine months away at best.

BOBBY: I've been there several times.

(Beat)

SUSANNAH: How many times?

BOBBY: What difference could that make?

SUSANNAH: None, but I'd like to know.

BOBBY: I can't say exactly.

SUSANNAH: That seems like a thing one would remember.

BOBBY: Since our troubles, the days have been running together in my mind. I don't want you worrying about this.

SUSANNAH: I feel strange about it.

BOBBY: You shouldn't. It means nothing.

SUSANNAH: I know, but…

BOBBY: Your father suggested it.

SUSANNAH: He did not.

BOBBY: Ask him. He knows what we're facing.

SUSANNAH: He never mentioned a word to me.

BOBBY: Why would he after you told him our secret? Things that happen in the quarters are as far away from the women under our protection as things that happen on the moon. Forget it.

SUSANNAH: I need to understand. I'll be calm.

BOBBY: Fine. Your father introduced me to a broker from Mississippi. He pays top dollar for wenches as long as they're showing.

SUSANNAH: The bucks should do this work.

BOBBY: The bucks aren't producing. Maybe they're playing tricks. I don't know. What I know is that we need a great deal of capital quickly.

SUSANNAH: That doesn't mean you had to—

BOBBY: Yes, it did. I'm not going to fail.

SUSANNAH: Was it only you?

BOBBY: There were two wenches and five bucks. I can't see why you're so bothered. There was no intimacy. This was a sacrifice. Think of it as husbandry.

SUSANNAH: My father never contemplated anything like this.

BOBBY: Yes, he has. I suspect your brothers as well.

*(*SUSANNAH *shakes her head "no".)*

BOBBY: Even a casual look around their home confirms it.

*(*SUSANNAH *slaps* BOBBY.*)*

SUSANNAH: It's not true. Take it back.

BOBBY: I don't mean to be crude.

SUSANNAH: Don't you mean cruel and mendacious? I feel like I'm going to be sick.

BOBBY: Do you want me to be part of your family or not? The only alternative I see is Dan Henry's way.

SUSANNAH: Sell them and start over?

BOBBY: Could you accept that? Could they?

SUSANNAH: You know the answer.

BOBBY: I went first before the bucks so I'm clean. That's a reasonable worry.

SUSANNAH: I don't want to hear this.

BOBBY: I got that advice from your oldest brother.

SUSANNAH: You won't even know which one's yours.

BOBBY: What difference could that possibly make? They'll belong to us for only a short time before they're launched into the world.

SUSANNAH: You're not including the ones I inherited from James, god rest his soul?

BOBBY: Strange time to bring up your late husband.

SUSANNAH: I don't like to press the point, but any thing that issues from them belongs to me by rights.

BOBBY: I believe dower property should be shared equally between husband and wife, under the stewardship of the husband of course.

SUSANNAH: Beloved if something happened to you, the ones you fathered would go to our male children. Consider what might happen to me then.

BOBBY: Our children would take care of you. I would train them to that.

*(*BOBBY *tenderly takes* SUSANNAH*'s hands.)*

SUSANNAH: There have been cases—

BOBBY: Tell me about them later. Take my last things off.

*(*BOBBY *stands before* SUSANNAH *naked, then reaches for her.)*

SUSANNAH: Let me bathe you first.

BOBBY: Now.

(BOBBY takes SUSANNAH to the floor for sex.)

(End scene)

Scene 7

(A cradle has been added to the room. A small pile of leftover wood is stacked near it. BOBBY sits at the table, his head in his hands.)

(The bedroom door is slightly ajar. A sliver of light comes from it. SUSANNAH is giving birth inside. She begins to quietly weep.)

BOBBY: Oh, god.

(SUSANNAH cries out. BOBBY rushes to the door. It slams shut. He kicks it.)

BOBBY: Do something for her!!

(A tiny bit of steam filters from the room. BOBBY paces to the other side of the room.)

BOBBY: The stench. It's worse than the slaughter.
(He opens the window.)

(The keening of unseen slave women from the quarters. It's unclear whether from celebration or mourning.)

BOBBY: Like animals. Quiet!!

(The slave women don't stop singing. Their voices mingle with SUSANNAH's quiet sobs.)

BOBBY: Calm down. Calm. Down. All is in God's hands. No one can challenge what he ordains. I've nothing to fear. But I do. Suddenly I'm aware of all there is to fear in the world. I fear it for the babe. What kind of father can I be when I am so flawed? I can barely keep Susannah and myself safe, now there's a helpless babe. All depending on me. The weight.

(Beat)

Flight. I should flee. Run as far and fast… Back to New Jersey? No, west. There's freedom there. I can remake myself.

*(*BOBBY*'s new born son wails. He stands slowly. A moment of reverence)*

BOBBY: I'm a man.

(The door opens. BOBBY *runs inside.)*

(End scene)

Scene 8

(Barely two weeks after the baby's birth. SUSANNAH *rocks the cradle.* BOBBY *enters. He drops his valise and goes to his wife and son.)*

SUSANNAH: Shhh. My aunt just got him down to sleep.

*(*BOBBY *puts his arms around* SUSANNAH*. They speak softly.)*

BOBBY: It's late. He's still fitful?

SUSANNAH: Aunt May says it's the colic.

BOBBY: He should get over that in no time. Where is she?

SUSANNAH: Gone to bed. She expected I'd want a moment alone with my husband.

BOBBY: She was right. It's good to be home.

SUSANNAH: You were missed.

BOBBY: It was only two nights.

SUSANNAH: And three days.

BOBBY: When the governor calls, one has to answer. It's an honor.

SUSANNAH: I'm deliriously proud of you. My husband's going to be an important man.

BOBBY: As soon as your lying-in's over, I'll have you on my arm at home and in town. But until then, this is contentment.

SUSANNAH: You are going to be a great patriarch.

BOBBY: He's the best gift I've ever been given. I'll always be in your debt.

SUSANNAH: I don't want you to see me as an obligation.

BOBBY: Forgive my poor choice of words. Sometimes language fails me.

SUSANNAH: How was the meeting?

BOBBY: Grand.

SUSANNAH: Tell me everything. What were the ladies wearing?

BOBBY: I couldn't say.

SUSANNAH: You never remember anything important.

BOBBY: Wouldn't you be angry if I did remember?

SUSANNAH: Maybe. Tell me what you do recall.

BOBBY: My room was well appointed. Royal blue. The finest carpentry and a feather bed. The meals were excellent.

SUSANNAH: Better than mine?

BOBBY: Absolutely not.

SUSANNAH: But fancy?

BOBBY: Oh my, yes. The boar was exceptional. In the evenings, the governor served a fine lager with which he was most liberal.

SUSANNAH: It sounds like there was the best of everything.

BOBBY: It was. I got the distinct impression that the governor is eyeing me for an appointment.

SUSANNAH: Did he say anything to that effect?

BOBBY: No, but Dan Henry seems to think—

SUSANNAH: Was James there, too?

BOBBY: We sat together.

SUSANNAH: I had a feeling those miscreants might be at the bottom of this.

BOBBY: Didn't I mention they were going?

SUSANNAH: You did not. I guess it must've slipped your mind.

BOBBY: How can you feel so strongly against them? You've known them all your life.

SUSANNAH: I've been acquainted with typhoid all my life and don't feel particularly warmly towards it either.

BOBBY: You now, my darling, are exaggerating for effect. Both made a real contribution to the discussions. James, in particular, has made a careful study of Indian country.

SUSANNAH: What else went on?

BOBBY: After we discussed the details of the new treaty last night, the governor let the Indians bring their wives to dinner.

SUSANNAH: What an insult.

BOBBY: To whom?

SUSANNAH: Every wife who was there. Can you imagine receiving an invitation to Columbia, putting on your best finery and finding a squaw next to you at dinner?

*(*BOBBY *laughs.)*

BOBBY: You'll be relieved to learn they were quite properly turned out.

SUSANNAH: Whose doing was that I wonder?

BOBBY: I saw very little difference between them and our women.

SUSANNAH: According to whose standard? You menfolk, please forgive me, aren't the always the best judge.

BOBBY: I'm not suggesting they are in any sense your equals.

SUSANNAH: That's a relief. Because they lack morality and refinement.

BOBBY: They managed to capture the appearance. That is something. Perhaps a sign that they may be able to seize some of the opportunities for progress that lie before them.

SUSANNAH: If I'd been there, something would have been said.

BOBBY: They were seated away from the men and the real wives. And so quiet, we barely knew they were there.

SUSANNAH: That's not the point and you know it. Inviting them at all puts them on the same level. I suspect the squaws knew that. Poor things were probably uncomfortable, but too scared to say anything.

BOBBY: All the same, everything turned out well. It was really engaging. I'd never thought about the significance of fishing treaties. Balancing our needs with the Cherokees.

SUSANNAH: I don't see why the state's revisiting those old treaties anyway.

BOBBY: It's important.

SUSANNAH: For what reasons, I cannot imagine. For goodness sake, what's done is done. The Cherokee lost and thank goodness. Everyone should accept it and make the best of things.

BOBBY: It's a matter of fairness. The original treaties never specified things as they should have done.

SUSANNAH: Yet and still, everyone's been fishing for forever and things have been fine. Bonnets or not bonnets, they are ungrateful.

BOBBY: The Cherokee didn't ask for this meeting. It was our men from Beaufort wanting greater access to the waterways.

SUSANNAH: Then they should have it.

BOBBY: If you were governor, everything would be so much simpler.

SUSANNAH: Well, it would.

BOBBY: You, my dear, are a treat.

SUSANNAH: Of course you men folk know best, but it seems to me that all these "issues" require is a bit of common sense.

(BOBBY *pats his lap.* SUSANNAH *sits on it.)*

SUSANNAH: I forgot. I have news.

BOBBY: Is it serious?

SUSANNAH: My aunt's needed back home.

BOBBY: When?

SUSANNAH: Uncle Thaddeus needs her as soon as possible. He's struggling, poor thing. They haven't got any household help. He's only the one hired man to help him.

BOBBY: Who's going to look after you?

SUSANNAH: It's all arranged. Uncle's going to send old Lucy. She looked after me sometimes when I was a girl.

BOBBY: Do you think she's fit for the job?

SUSANNAH: She's been well taken care by my family for years. She's got plenty of use left in her.

BOBBY: If you're comfortable with it.

SUSANNAH: I am. There's no need to run tattling to Dan Henry or James. Lucy's delighted to come serve her old charge.

BOBBY: That's good to know. And tattling hadn't crossed my mind.

SUSANNAH: Progress. I'll make you into a Beasley yet.

BOBBY: Do you trust her?

SUSANNAH: Completely. She knows exactly what to do.

BOBBY: How many has she had?

SUSANNAH: Ten or eleven?

BOBBY: When would we have to return her?

SUSANNAH: It's up to us. Uncle hinted that he might turn her over to us. He and aunt want
(Imitates her uncle)
"To give the young couple a good start."

BOBBY: The people here, your family, our family are so kind.
(He hides his impending tears. He goes to the stack of leftover wood.)
I'm going to start on a small bed for our lad.

SUSANNAH: Get Sammy to help.

BOBBY: I want to build it with my own two hands.

(End scene)

Scene 9

(After dinner a few weeks later. BOBBY *waits at the table.)*

(His wife SUSANNAH *walks in slowly from the nursery, buttoning her shirt. He looks at her hopefully. She shakes her head, "no".)*

BOBBY: Why doesn't he cry?

SUSANNAH: Too weak.
(She touches her breasts.)
They've just dried up. I can't—I don't feel anything. Why aren't they full?

BOBBY: I'll get the midwife.

SUSANNAH: It's no use. She was just here. I'm trying everything I can think of. Touching myself.

BOBBY: Maybe it's sinful, doing that. No, that can't be. I pray over you in your sleep.

SUSANNAH: You do?

BOBBY: Reverend Hull told me to pronounce blessings over my household. It's worked. Look at how we're prospering.

SUSANNAH: Except for me not being able to feed our son.

*(*SUSANNAH *buries herself in* BOBBY*'s arms.)*

BOBBY: There's not a thing wrong with you, Mrs. Hawkins.

SUSANNAH: Then why did it take us so long to conceive? And now…

BOBBY: Stop that. Doc said there was nothing wrong with either one of us. God's timing is all. Tell me your day. Maybe I can discern a pattern.

SUSANNAH: I tried feeding him first thing as soon as I've finished my devotion. Then before I begin my work for the day. Before lunch ... I try throughout the day.

BOBBY: Did you try moving around while nursing?

SUSANNAH: From side to side, sitting, standing. Nothing works. Nothing. He's getting so thin and pale.

BOBBY: What's Lucy been doing?

SUSANNAH: It's not her fault.

BOBBY: She doesn't seem like she's helping. She's supposed to tend to you.

SUSANNAH: She does.

*(*BOBBY *takes the whip down from the wall and grooms it.)*

BOBBY: Maybe she needs a touch—

SUSANNAH: Don't. I can't manage without her.

BOBBY: She's had a whole litter. She must know what to do. She's going to tell it.
(He slaps the whip against his palm.)

SUSANNAH: Bobby, please. She's only got one good eye left. She can't take another beating. She wouldn't be any good to me at all. If it comes to it, I'll take care of her myself. She helped rear me.

BOBBY: All right. But say the word if things aren't right, you hear? There's something about her I don't trust.

SUSANNAH: You don't know her as I do.

BOBBY: I trust my gut.

SUSANNAH: Let me speak to her.

BOBBY: Is anything paining you?

SUSANNAH: No. I wish it did. Maybe it would be a sign things were about to get better.

BOBBY: Did you remember to take your treatments?

SUSANNAH: I drink thistle and barley every day. My skin reeks of them.

BOBBY: What about the oats?

(SUSANNAH nods.)

SUSANNAH: He spit up the goat milk I gave him. I thought I'd have a kind of instinct, but I'm lost.

BOBBY: Someone has to know. I'll go to the midwife—

SUSANNAH: Don't go telling everyone our business.

BOBBY: Why?

SUSANNAH: What if they're cursing us?

(BOBBY and SUSANNAH's son screams. She rushes to the nursery.)

SUSANNAH: Get doc. And the midwife.

BOBBY: I'll have to pass through town. People will see.

(SUSANNAH hesitates, then another agonizing wail.)

SUSANNAH: *(O S)* Go!

(End scene)

Scene 10

(The next night. BOBBY studies the ledger. He holds the African style leather necklace as if it were a rosary. He hides it when SUSANNAH staggers in from the nursery.)

BOBBY: Is he asleep?

SUSANNAH: The medicine's working.

BOBBY: But he can only take it for a few days.

(SUSANNAH sits heavily.)

BOBBY: You're exhausted.

SUSANNAH: You must be as well.

BOBBY: At least I'm able to get out.

SUSANNAH: I miss the fresh air.

BOBBY: Just a little while longer.

SUSANNAH: I was so looking forward to the lying in. I thought my baby and I would become close. Instead, this. I'm skittish and afraid all the time.

BOBBY: It's natural given the circumstances. You have to hang on.

SUSANNAH: You're right.

*(*BOBBY *retrieves the ledger.)*

SUSANNAH: Figures at this hour? Can't they wait?

BOBBY: Doc is right. We've got to find a way to pay for a wet nurse. If that doesn't work, we'll mortgage the property and take the boy north for treatment.

SUSANNAH: A mortgage could mean we lose everything.

BOBBY: Not necessarily.

SUSANNAH: The country's still in the middle of a panic.

BOBBY: Then so be it. Our son comes first.

SUSANNAH: There have been generations of Beasleys on this land. If we lost it, I can't even bear to think of it.

BOBBY: A future's more than land. Junior's our future.

SUSANNAH: Do you know what we'd be giving up?

BOBBY: We'd manage.

SUSANNAH: What about your ambitions? You have money, but without land you couldn't stand for office.

BOBBY: I can't think about that now.

SUSANNAH: I'd rather cut my own throat than lose Junior, but we could—

BOBBY: Don't say any more.

SUSANNAH: I—

BOBBY: Not another syllable. Some words let loose into the world bring destruction. They etch like acid and can't be washed away.

SUSANNAH: Do you know what this is taking from me? Look at me. Look at me!

BOBBY: You'll recover.

SUSANNAH: It kills me to even…we've had one. Everyone says it's much easier the second time.

BOBBY: *(Repulsed)* No.

SUSANNAH: Look at how many our parents lost. They found a way to go on.

BOBBY: Stop.

SUSANNAH: What if it's god's will?

*(*BOBBY *pushes* SUSANNAH *against the wall.)*

BOBBY: If anything happens to my son by omission or commission. If a single hair on his head— Do you understand?

SUSANNAH: What if he doesn't take to the wet nurse? That happens.

BOBBY: Say that you understand.

SUSANNAH: If we spend everything and it's still not enough? Please explain what's wrong with considering every possibility. However terrible.

*(*BOBBY *releases* SUSANNAH.*)*

BOBBY: Callousness isn't limited to your brothers.

SUSANNAH: Do you have any idea of what it cost me to say this, let alone think it?

BOBBY: This isn't even your fault. You've never had to sacrifice, even with your family's troubles. The town can set its clock by your shopping trip to Atlanta. Hats, dresses. Who knows what all else you and your friends get up to.

SUSANNAH: We can't turn on each other.

BOBBY: You spend a fortune, and I've never begrudged one cent. I doubt your father did either.

SUSANNAH: My family has to set a certain standard.

BOBBY: If keeping up appearances are your primary concern, you're not strong enough to condemn your own issue to death. We'll speak no more of this.

SUSANNAH: I love him, too.

BOBBY: Everyone's life comes at a cost, including yours. I'm willing to pay for my son's. Don't make me compare prices.

SUSANNAH: What about the farm equipment?

BOBBY: Everything we have we use. We've nothing extra. Even if we did, it wouldn't bring in anything close to what we need.

SUSANNAH: That much?

BOBBY: Wet nurses command a high price.

SUSANNAH: If we hadn't sold off the women.

BOBBY: We'd be in an even worse position.

SUSANNAH: You have to let me keep the ones in the house. I can hardly manage as it is. Can you spare one from the fields?

BOBBY: A buck would bring in more, but they produce in the fields. The harvest's about to come in. I don't think we should chance it.

SUSANNAH: All right.

BOBBY: It has to be Lucy. Do you think your aunt and uncle would allow it?

SUSANNAH: I'm sure of it. I'll tell Lucy to put her things together.

BOBBY: Wait until we find a buyer. I don't want to spook the quarters.

SUSANNAH: Ours would never even dare dream of rebellion, of any kind. Those are the fears of your friends.

BOBBY: Perhaps.

SUSANNAH: Let me help. Daddy knows the *Clarion*'s editor. He could ensure favorable placement of our advertisement.

BOBBY: I'd rather deliver her to auction. I've been assured that's the best way to get the price we need.

SUSANNAH: I'd like to come.

BOBBY: Why?

SUSANNAH: To support you. The town still doesn't consider you a local. Besides, I grew up with her. I should send her off.

BOBBY: We'll take the carriage.

SUSANNAH: It only seats two.

BOBBY: It's more comfortable than a coach. We still have to think of your condition.

SUSANNAH: Any Lucy?

BOBBY: As long as the horse can take the weight, she can ride with the driver. Or walk behind us. It's not that far.

SUSANNAH: That would be fine.

BOBBY: Promise me if it gets to be too much, you'll let me send you home.

SUSANNAH: I give you my word. I'll be strong. She's been with me since the beginning. The family we bought her from died out. She's my obligation now.

BOBBY: Should we leave junior with your sister-in-law?

SUSANNAH: He belongs with us. It's important that he see from the beginning how to treat those who belong to us. Lucy came when I was six. Her daughter Hetty was my first. How we loved each other. She'd run to get whatever I asked her for. If she didn't, I'd give her a love kick.

BOBBY: That is a long history.

SUSANNAH: One worthy of honor.

BOBBY: We travel in three days.

SUSANNAH: I'll be ready.

(End scene)

Scene 11

(Dawn, the day of the auction. BOBBY *holds his son with trepidation.)*

BOBBY: I'm afraid you'll break. That your bones are too brittle to support you. Do you know my greatest fear? That I'll have to put you down. The way we do horses. Your mother pretends she could release you to death. In the end, I'm the only one with the strength for that. I don't know if I have the right. You're our miracle.

(Beat)

None of this has to come to pass if you hold on. If you do that, daddy's going to fix everything. You'll start picking up weight and gaining strength. You'll be the eldest brother. We'll joke about this when you and I go fishing. At church when the preacher's not looking, your mother will turn, see us smiling at each other and wonder. We'll have a bond no one can challenge. I'll send you north for school. You'll come back to help me when I'm old. Staying is a decision. Decide to stay. I believe the maker gives us some control over our destinies. Bend your heart to this side of the mortal coil.

*(*SUSANNAH *enters and rushes to* BOBBY *and son.)*

SUSANNAH: Give him to me. You're holding him too tightly.

*(*BOBBY *does.)*

SUSANNAH: I hope you understand. I couldn't bear it if…

BOBBY: I truly understand.

*(*BOBBY *dangles the calfskin pouch with the fingertip to entrance his son.* SUSANNAH *grabs for it. He playfully keeps it away from her.)*

SUSANNAH: He's not old enough to play with it yet. I am.

BOBBY: Mine, then his.

(End scene)

Scene 12

(That evening. BOBBY *carries* SUSANNAH *across the threshold.)*

BOBBY: Are you all right to walk?

*(*SUSANNAH *steps down.)*

SUSANNAH: Just a dizzy spell. Too much excitement.

BOBBY: Someone had a good time.

SUSANNAH: The hawkers and music. I wasn't expecting. It's like a party. Did you see what Alice Mae had on? Maroon really favors her. I wish I could wear colors that dark.

BOBBY: I'll tell you a little secret. Business can be a great deal of fun.

SUSANNAH: So I see. I was shocked to see Widow Hutchinson. I'd heard she was under the weather.

BOBBY: I hope she hasn't fallen on hard times.

SUSANNAH: Do you think?

BOBBY: Dan Henry said it was unusual to sell two lots at this point in the season. I think I'll call on her.

SUSANNAH: Don't be too obvious. I'd hate to embarrass her. I've always admired the pride she has about herself.

BOBBY: I'll consult with the other deacons on how to handle the situation.

SUSANNAH: You're becoming one of us.

BOBBY: All I needed was time.

SUSANNAH: Willing hands and a good heart.

BOBBY: Do I make you proud?

(SUSANNAH *nods.)*

SUSANNAH: Maybe we shouldn't say anything. Let's give it a little time and see if she brings it up.

BOBBY: It's not right to let her struggle. From everything I've heard Asa was a real good man.

SUSANNAH: Daddy said he was the best.

BOBBY: It would be an honor to do for his widow.

SUSANNAH: I feel sorry for women whose husbands aren't like you.

BOBBY: I'd want others to do the same for you. Everyone deserves their dignity.

SUSANNAH: Nothing's ever going to happen to you. I decree it. If it does, you'll just live on through Junior, then Moses, Elijah, Daniel, Hamish, Rachel and Sarah.

BOBBY: You already have names picked out?

SUSANNAH: And birth order. A good wife's supposed to be prepared.

BOBBY: I've rarely found you wanting. I write all my bachelor friends that they should marry southern girls. They know how to make a life.

SUSANNAH: We certainly try.

BOBBY: Agreed. Not to change the subject, but I have a surprise.

SUSANNAH: I love surprises. I pledge to love whatever it is until my dying day.

*(*SUSANNAH *puts her hands over her eyes.* BOBBY *hands her the title for the new wet nurse.)*

SUSANNAH: What is it? Tell me.

BOBBY: The wet nurse is yours.

SUSANNAH: Is this the title? I've never held anything this valuable in my hands before.

BOBBY: Except Junior.

SUSANNAH: Of course.
(She playfully taps him on the arm.)
You're not saying it, but this keeps my stock at the same number. Lucy was ours, well really aunt and uncle's. This nurse would be all mine.

BOBBY: I was hoping you'd notice.

SUSANNAH: I surely have.

BOBBY: When junior's done, you can keep her for your own particular use.

SUSANNAH: This means the world. I'm going to rename her Grace Ellen.

BOBBY: Ellen for your nana. Why Grace?

SUSANNAH: Because every time I call for her, it'll remind me that you're God's gift to me. Everything's perfect. Lucy gets to stay in our Carolina.

BOBBY: For $725 when the auctioneer thought she might only fetch $700.

SUSANNAH: After so many years with us, she gets to die under the same sky as her children. My mother would've been so pleased.

BOBBY: All's well that ends well.

(End scene)

Scene 13

(Night. SUSANNAH *ladles soup into bowls. She is agitated.* BOBBY *enters from the nursery.)*

BOBBY: Our boy's thriving.

SUSANNAH: That he is.

BOBBY: I love seeing him getting brown and strong in the sun.

SUSANNAH: Think of how weak he was. That doesn't even feel real now. It's like it was all a bad dream.

BOBBY: A bad dream we've put firmly behind us. I can finally play with him like I want to. Pinch his fat little cheeks, bite his toes. What a difference.

*(*BOBBY *notices something with* SUSANNAH.*)*

BOBBY: Is anything wrong?

SUSANNAH: It might be my imagination, but I've been wondering about Grace Ellen.

BOBBY: What a godsend.

SUSANNAH: Who does she think she is?

BOBBY: Did something happen?

SUSANNAH: She acts like she's his mother, flouncing around. This morning she nearly pushed me aside, when he started crying.

BOBBY: To give him the teat?

(SUSANNAH nods.)

BOBBY: I told her to feed him as soon as even looks like he's hungry. That's how he's been getting better.

SUSANNAH: Does that mean she doesn't have to show me respect? She should know better.

BOBBY: I'll speak to her.

SUSANNAH: She's mine. I should be the one to do it.

BOBBY: It's your right. But if I may, you shouldn't do anything too harsh. It might damage her flow.

SUSANNAH: Should I coo to her softly? It's harder for me to establish my authority than you.

BOBBY: I haven't noticed any problems.

SUSANNAH: There are some things only a woman would see.

BOBBY: Try taking away something she likes. She seems to take a lot of pride in her hair. Take her comb. But remember, if we're too harsh with them—

SUSANNAH: If we're too harsh with them, what? That's sounds like Dan Henry again.

BOBBY: I'm not Dan's mouthpiece. I have my own thoughts. I'm worried about her trying to run away. James lost two last month.

SUSANNAH: Because he was imprudent.

BOBBY: I'm not sure about that. I just assumed they would let her newborn come with her.

SUSANNAH: She should know better than to expect such a thing.

BOBBY: Still with the ones James lost, it's worrying.

SUSANNAH: Isn't that what your hound is for? He has to be good for something besides eating.

BOBBY: He's never tracked a runaway.

SUSANNAH: Show that dog you mean business. When the time comes, get him out there and let him earn his keep.

BOBBY: *(Warmly)* I'll thank you not to get between a man and his dog. That relationship's sacred.

(SUSANNAH laughs.)

BOBBY: We should consider letting Grace Ellen go back to her people at Christmas. They work harder if allowed some liberty. Else what incentive do they have?

SUSANNAH: Their incentive's to stay far from Louisiana or Mississippi. They're not like us. Life's much harder for them there. I, for one, think that means Grace Ellen should be more grateful.

BOBBY: You know my sentiments. I trust you do to what's right. What smells good?

SUSANNAH: Brunswick stew.

BOBBY: My favorite.

SUSANNAH: After I put the baby down, I went out to shoot, so we have squirrel.

BOBBY: That's my little huntress.
(He smells the dish.)
Delicious.

SUSANNAH: It's how we belles keep our men happy.

(End scene)

Scene 14

(Early evening. SUSANNAH *enters from outside, wearing a dressing gown, with barely perceptible blood streaks.)*

SUSANNAH: Bobby? Are you home? I'm back from quarters.
(She holds a clump of Grace Ellen's hair. It still has a bit of flesh attached. She sits and studies it for a long time.)
(Finally, she singes it. When she's done, she folds it inside her own locket with great satisfaction.)
All as it should be, Grace Ellen. All as it should be.
(She brushes hair and ashes from her hands onto the table.)
One less thing for our Bobby to deal with when he gets home.

(An almost imperceptible sound of slave women with BOBBY*'s voice mixed in among them.* SUSANNAH *covers her ears and runs into the bedroom.)*

(End scene)

Scene 15

(The same night. BOBBY *enters. His pants undone. He quickly buttons them, but allows his finger to linger on the dampness of his crotch for a moment.)*

BOBBY: There's still heat. Be gone from me. It doesn't matter. I am clean.
(He retrieves junior from his crib.)
(Sings)

Bah, Bah, black Sheep, Have you any wool? Yes, merry have I. Three bags full. Two for my master. One for my dame. None for the little boy who cries in the lane.

(Speaks)

Sweet dreams, Enoch Robert Hawkins, Jr. Hurry and grow up. I could use the company. I feel so all alone.

(He sits at the table and finds the hair and ashes. He rubs them between his fingers, thinks for a long time, then decides not to see them. He wipes his hands clean.)

Everything's going to be all right.

(He returns his son to the crib, then finds the plate SUSANNAH *left for him.)*

Everything is all right.

(He sits and unwraps his food.)

(End scene)

Scene 16

(Late night. BOBBY *is at the door, quietly putting on his boots. He whistles softly for his hound. A soft growl in response.* SUSANNAH *enters.)*

BOBBY: I didn't mean to wake you.

SUSANNAH: I wasn't asleep. I never completely rest when you're out of our bed.

BOBBY: I'll be back soon.

SUSANNAH: Why do you keep going back there?

BOBBY: You don't know where I'm going.

SUSANNAH: You should come home smelling sweet like hay. You never do.

BOBBY: My presence is necessary.

SUSANNAH: For what reason?

BOBBY: To check on things.

SUSANNAH: Do you imagine I don't know? I see the looks and hear the sighs.

BOBBY: There are lots of things you decide not to see. Let this be one of them.

SUSANNAH: Nearly every wench in the quarters is with child.

BOBBY: Then our plan's working.

(He opens the door.)

SUSANNAH: It's past eleven. It's dangerous. There are snakes—

BOBBY: Go to bed.

SUSANNAH: What do you expect people to think?

BOBBY: I'll let you concern yourself with that. I'm persuaded that no one's the least bit concerned with us. We're all still busy trying to recover from the floods.

SUSANNAH: The land's fully planted. Our farm's turned the corner. Before god, what excuse do you think you have?

BOBBY: I don't believe I need one. This falls within my scope of responsibilities. You, yourself, can attest to how dutiful I am.

SUSANNAH: Duty? Or desire? That is what I fear.

(BOBBY goes for the door. SUSANNAH takes a whip off the wall.)

BOBBY: Put it back.

SUSANNAH: I'm going with you.

BOBBY: I think you will not.

SUSANNAH: "Behold, thy maid Hagar is in thy hand; do to her as it pleaseth you. Then Sarai dealt harshly with Hagar…" This is my home. I have the same rights as Sarai. It is ordained.

BOBBY: In the story, Hagar fled. Our wenches can't flee. Hagar was under god's protection. He never abandoned her.

SUSANNAH: But her seed sowed long lasting division.

BOBBY: I don't pretend to know the future, but everything on these properties are under my protection. The wenches bring a better return than rice ever could. Things will continue as they have been.

*(*SUSANNAH *clenches the whip.)*

SUSANNAH: If you go, they taste this.

BOBBY: No, she won't.

SUSANNAH: You mean Grace Ellen?

*(*BOBBY *walks to the door.* SUSANNAH *flails at him.)*

SUSANNAH: You said you'd never abandon me. What do you call this?

*(*BOBBY *pins* SUSANNAH, *but she still struggles.)*

BOBBY: Don't make me do this. It's not the kind of man I want to be.

*(*SUSANNAH *quiets.* BOBBY *lets her go.)*

BOBBY: I'll be back.

SUSANNAH: I won't let you shame my family's name.

*(*SUSANNAH *lifts the whip to strike.* BOBBY *knocks it out of her hand, inadvertently knocking her to the ground. They scramble for it.)*

(He wrests it away and holds it over her head. She raises her hands defensively.)

BOBBY: Put your hands down.

*(*SUSANNAH *does. He viciously whips the ground next to her until she screams.* BOBBY *covers her mouth.)*

BOBBY: Our families' survival hinges on me. Me. Everyone is depending on me: your brothers, Dan Henry, the deacons, James.

SUSANNAH: It's made you prideful.

BOBBY: It's made me clear. I'll do what I have to. That includes disciplining you.
(Whispers)
I assure you. I don't want to.

SUSANNAH: Then…

*(*BOBBY *puts his finger to his lips to indicate silence, then walks out.)*

SUSANNAH: Don't go.
(She bites her locket that holds Grace Ellen's flesh in frustration and anger.)

(End scene)

Scene 17

(The evening after the couple's first party. The chairs and table have been shoved against the walls. BOBBY *and* SUSANNAH *sit, pleasantly exhausted.)*

BOBBY: We needed this.
(He kisses his wife's hand.)
You're a wonderful hostess.

SUSANNAH: All I needed was the opportunity to prove myself. The end of my lying-in was the perfect chance.

BOBBY: You make me proud. There hasn't been a cross word between us. This is the kind of peace I want for our family.

*(*SUSANNAH *rests her head on* BOBBY*'s shoulder.)*

BOBBY: We need to have company more often. We're too much to ourselves out here. That probably accounts for some of the strain between us.

SUSANNAH: I'm used to the country. But you're from town, I should've realized…

BOBBY: I never thought of it, but I think you must be right.

SUSANNAH: However, we may want to keep our privacy awhile longer.

BOBBY: Why's that?

SUSANNAH: Junior wants a baby sister.

BOBBY: How can you tell?

SUSANNAH: Tonight he kept pointing at other babies, especially the girls.

BOBBY: Father and son are on one accord.

SUSANNAH: It would mean everything to my father. I so want you to be friends, not just allies. I hope you noticed my brothers went out of their way to be gracious to Dan Henry and James.

BOBBY: I noticed. A minor miracle, that.

SUSANNAH: They did that for you.

BOBBY: They recognize that a man has to have friends.

SUSANNAH: So tonight was a success all the way around.

BOBBY: Your aunt can't get enough of Junior. I thought they'd swallow him whole.

SUSANNAH: Do you think he favors her?

BOBBY: It's hard to say. He changes so much every day.

SUSANNAH: I thought his hair would stay blonde, but it's darkening. Grace Ellen might be letting him stay in the sun too long.

BOBBY: Remember what a blessing she is. It really helps to have an extra pair of hands.

SUSANNAH: After Junior's weaned, I think she should go to the fields.

BOBBY: That's a ways off. Why don't we decide when we reach that juncture?

SUSANNAH: What's wrong with deciding now? I think the fields give a certain discipline. She'd benefit from that. She could always come back after we have our second. She'd have more appreciation.

BOBBY: I'm not sure…

SUSANNAH: When she was bringing me my lavender water, she strutted into our room like she owned the place.

BOBBY: She always calls me Master Hawkins.

SUSANNAH: But with a certain tone. A certain knowing.

BOBBY: I respectfully disagree. Be thankful. Lucy was too old to do half of what she does.

SUSANNAH: Lucy knew her place. Grace Ellen's trying to bewitch my entire household.

BOBBY: Now why would she do that?

SUSANNAH: For spite, since I disciplined her. For all we know, she might be working roots against us.

BOBBY: We've had a good night. Let's shake off this bad mood.
(He stands and holds his arms open.)
I'd like to hold my bride.

SUSANNAH: Changing the subject?

BOBBY: Yes, ma'am.

*(*BOBBY *pulls* SUSANNAH *to her feet and embraces her.)*

BOBBY: No one could ever have explained how sweet the tenderness of matrimony can feel.

SUSANNAH: Or how painful the disagreements.

BOBBY: Disagreements only make the good times sweeter.

SUSANNAH: It's a happiness too delicate to put into words. I'm terrified to do something to destroy it. Everything's so fragile.

BOBBY: That's not going to happen. I won't let it.

SUSANNAH: You are strength.

BOBBY: You get ready for bed. I'm going out with the hound.

SUSANNAH: Why?

BOBBY: Just for a moment, to clear my head.

(SUSANNAH puts her head on BOBBY's chest.)

SUSANNAH: Smell the same when you come back.

BOBBY: Of course. Don't be silly.
(He exits.)

(End scene)

Scene 18

(SUSANNAH sits at the table chuckling. Her hair is in a new style.)

(BOBBY enters. He stands in the doorway enjoying her good spirits for a moment.)

BOBBY: It's great to see you in such good spirits.

SUSANNAH: Junior's first tooth came in.

BOBBY: Everything's happening so fast.

SUSANNAH: He bit Grace Ellen's teat. He made her bleed.

BOBBY: Is she all right?

SUSANNAH: You should be asking if Junior's all right. What if some of that blood got into his system?

BOBBY: I can't see it would do him any harm.

SUSANNAH: Who knows what makes them that color? Maybe all it takes is one drop.

BOBBY: That's silly.

SUSANNAH: Are you an expert on this subject, too?

BOBBY: Perhaps it's time to start weaning him.

SUSANNAH: Not yet.

BOBBY: Well, you women are the experts on these things.

SUSANNAH: A man with a brilliant political future shouldn't concern himself with trivial matters.
(She unveils a cake.)
To celebrate the tooth, I had Grace Ellen make a burnt leather cake. A gift baked a gift.

BOBBY: She must be all right then.

SUSANNAH: She fainted.

*(*SUSANNAH *sees* BOBBY*'s anxiety and makes him wait for an explanation.)*

SUSANNAH: I tended to her myself. Even Dan Henry and James would approve of her care. Your son hasn't see you all day.

BOBBY: Should I—?

SUSANNAH: I want you for myself to a few moments. Is that wrong?

BOBBY: No.

(BOBBY *takes* SUSANNAH*'s hand, but is a bit fidgety.)*

SUSANNAH: Don't you even dare think of going to see that wench. I left her with the older women. She'll be fine.

BOBBY: The cake looks inviting.

SUSANNAH: I know it's your favorite.

(BOBBY *tries it. He has to choke it down.)*

BOBBY: Mmmm. Delicious.

SUSANNAH: I think God will favor us with another bundle of joy very soon. I can feel it in my bones.

BOBBY: There's no hurry. We don't want to ill use you. Your body needs rest.

SUSANNAH: To be used for a higher purpose is a good thing. I embrace it.

BOBBY: We want the next one to be healthy.

SUSANNAH: Then come to me in the mornings and in the evenings when the sun goes down. We'll lie together—

BOBBY: Please, don't be crass.

SUSANNAH: I just want you to know that you are very much wanted by your wife and son. We need you.

BOBBY: In whatever ways we're blessed, I'll be satisfied.

(End scene)

Scene 19

(BOBBY *enters. He is startled to see blood streaks on the floor.* SUSANNAH *covers the crib.)*

SUSANNAH: *(Cheerful)* He's sleeping.

(BOBBY *peeks into the crib.* SUSANNAH *rubs his back. He subtly eases away from her touch.)*

BOBBY: Evening.

SUSANNAH: Evening.

(BOBBY *can't take his eyes off the blood.)*

SUSANNAH: How'd you do?

BOBBY: It was a good day. Productive. Our hard work's paying off.

SUSANNAH: Thank you for saying "our".

BOBBY: The good lord in his wisdom provides men helpmeets. He knew how critical your contributions would be.

SUSANNAH: Should we have another party to celebrate?

BOBBY: We're not completely out of the woods yet.

SUSANNAH: When we are, say the word. I can make preparations for a fete in no time. Until then, I can only admire your business acumen. You've made good on your promises.

BOBBY: It is truly a relief to have turned the corner. In less than a year I feel as if I'd aged ten.

SUSANNAH: You're still my handsome Yankee.

BOBBY: Has anything happened, beloved?

SUSANNAH: With what?

BOBBY: It looks like blood.

SUSANNAH: It is, my love.

BOBBY: Talk to me.

SUSANNAH: About?

BOBBY: Whose blood is it?

SUSANNAH: Are you worried?

BOBBY: Concerned.

SUSANNAH: She stepped out of line again.

BOBBY: Grace Ellen?

SUSANNAH: Who else? None of the others attempt to take liberties.

BOBBY: All those beatings must have made an impression.

SUSANNAH: I've never been inappropriate.

BOBBY: You're within your rights.

SUSANNAH: I'm not making it up about Grace Ellen. I am not.

BOBBY: What about the others?

SUSANNAH: I have a duty to instill discipline.

BOBBY: I'm worried. It's not healthy for you to get so agitated. Discipline is not the same thing as cruelty.

SUSANNAH: One example.

BOBBY: I find clumps of hair.

SUSANNAH: Hair grows back. You're gone a great deal. Do you have any idea of what goes on when you're not here?

BOBBY: I'm master. I depend on you to tell me the things that I miss.

SUSANNAH: Did you know Grace Ellen is with child?

(BOBBY *doesn't answer.)*

SUSANNAH: Dan Henry might not approve if he knew—

BOBBY: Dan Henry's a bachelor with an independent income. There's no way he can understand the challenges that continue to face us. Yes, I'm in sympathy with some of his ideas. But when there's a conflict between my ideals and my family, my loyalty's with my son and you. I hope that's enough to keep the peace.

SUSANNAH: It's not. Her focus is elsewhere. I'm surprised you don't see the implications. How can she serve if she's distracted by her own needs?

(BOBBY *uses his foot to wipe away some of the blood.)*

SUSANNAH: Some buck's been playing in the hen house. I want him found.

BOBBY: And what?

SUSANNAH: Dealt with.

BOBBY: I've been leasing her husband from time to time.

SUSANNAH: Since when?

BOBBY: He's called Solomon. He brings the child to see her. I thought it would calm her—

SUSANNAH: Oh!

BOBBY: And that that would put the tensions between you to rest.

SUSANNAH: Why didn't I know that?

BOBBY: Managing the fields is my business.

SUSANNAH: I should've been informed. I want their child sold. It will not grow up on Beasley land.

BOBBY: I will determine if business conditions warrant.

SUSANNAH: There are things I need for the house. We'll need the money.

BOBBY: Which things exactly?

SUSANNAH: I'll let you know.

BOBBY: I refuse to keep spoiling you. I'm warning you. You need to be careful. Not just you, but all the women in town.

SUSANNAH: I'm not responsible for them.

BOBBY: You're the first lady of this town. Take the responsibility that comes with it. People are noticing how much harm you're causing to the properties.

SUSANNAH: Who said that? No, I can guess.

BOBBY: There are too many missing teeth and broken bones and patchy scalps. We both know that Grace Ellen has had the worst of it. If you stop, they'll stop. Put this ridiculous jealousy or whatever it is behind you.

SUSANNAH: How could I be jealous of something—

BOBBY: Dan Henry and James have threatened to go to Columbia.

SUSANNAH: I'm sure their concern is something you find admirable.

BOBBY: They're planning ask the Governor for new laws that would tell owners in very precise terms how exactly we can discipline. Very precise indeed. How long, with what, when, and how often. Is that what you want?

SUSANNAH: They wouldn't dare. That's a total betrayal—

BOBBY: The only reason they haven't already gone is because I assured them—understand what that means, I gave them my word—you would stop.

SUSANNAH: No one can interfere with my god given—

BOBBY: We can't afford to run afoul of the law.

SUSANNAH: That law would never be enforced here.

BOBBY: Are you so certain Sheriff Carter would hesitate when he might be able to seize some property for himself? Look at me and tell me he wouldn't.

SUSANNAH: Sheriff wasn't always… The man has had his troubles.

BOBBY: And I have mine. Let me speak plainly. No longer care what's happened between you and Stop beating Grace Ellen. Stop beating her. With your fists, the whip. Don't put her fingers under the rocking chair. None of it. If you stop, the other wives will too.

(SUSANNAH salutes BOBBY.)

BOBBY: Clean this mess up and be quick about it. Even dogs know better than to lie in their own filth. Now!

(SUSANNAH begins. BOBBY watches her.)

(End scene)

Scene 20

(BOBBY enters and empties his pockets including his calf skin pouch onto the table.)

(SUSANNAH enters, sees the pouch, grabs it, then locks herself in the bedroom.)

BOBBY: Susannah!

BOBBY pounds on the door. No answer.

BOBBY: You're a child.

SUSANNAH: *(O S)* You're a monster to treat me this way. I'm your wife. You should withhold nothing from me. Nothing.

BOBBY: Bring me my son.

SUSANNAH: Not until you apologize.

(BOBBY kicks the door open. SUSANNAH whimpers. He closes the door.)

(End scene)

Scene 21

(Lunchtime, but the food's been forgotten.)

*(*BOBBY *and* SUSANNAH *stand on opposite sides of the room, a blood-soaked whip on the floor between them.)*

BOBBY: How did it get into your head to whip a buck?

SUSANNAH: I didn't like the way he looked at me.

BOBBY: What were you doing out there in the first place?

SUSANNAH: I was—

BOBBY: There's plenty for you to do here in the house. I absolutely forbid you to go out to the fields again. Can you imagine the scene it would've made if I had happened upon you?

SUSANNAH: This is our land together, isn't it?

BOBBY: Am I supposed to pretend you don't know that he's Grace Ellen's man?

SUSANNAH: Was he?

BOBBY: His owner's going to make me pay damages.

SUSANNAH: Refuse to pay.

BOBBY: I can't do that. The man is within his rights.

SUSANNAH: Nothing in the law forbids us from disciplining a slave, stranger, owned or leased.

BOBBY: You're losing control.

SUSANNAH: I'm gaining control by demanding respect.

BOBBY: You need time away. First thing in the morning I want you to pack your bags.

SUSANNAH: I'm not due to go to Atlanta for months.

BOBBY: You'll go early this year and stay for a while.

SUSANNAH: With Junior.

BOBBY: Without him.

SUSANNAH: Don't make me go.

BOBBY: Then behave yourself. I'm concerned about the changes I'm seeing. I won't hesitate to reverse my ruling on this.

SUSANNAH: You're always after me to grow and how do you put it? Develop my mind. That's exactly what I'm doing.

BOBBY: Fine. Do it less physically.

SUSANNAH: Junior crawled into bed with Grace Ellen. Would you like to take this opportunity?

BOBBY: No, I would not.

SUSANNAH: Will you be going to the quarters?

BOBBY: Perhaps. Or maybe I'll stay here, keeping an eye on things. I'll let you know what I decide. Lunch.

They ease around the whip to assume their lunchtime positions.

(End scene)

Scene 22

(Beautiful, pastoral light bathes SUSANNAH *as she braids a cross out of wild flowers.)*

(The walls, the floor and her dress are blood splattered. Scraps of well-worn gingham fabric are strewn about. Bloody footprints lead out the back door.)

*(*BOBBY *enters. A moment of silence then the slave women begin humming a spiritual offstage.)*

BOBBY: Dead or living?

*(*SUSANNAH *braids more quickly and sloppily.)*

SUSANNAH: *(Sings)* Going forth with weeping, sowing for the Master. Though the loss sustained our spirit often grieves—

BOBBY: Susannah, I know you hear me. Dead—

SUSANNAH: *(Sings)* Bringing in the sheaves, bringing in the sheaves. We shall come rejoicing, bringing in the sheaves.

BOBBY: Stop it.

SUSANNAH: *(Sings)* Bringing in—

BOBBY: Silence!
(He closes the curtains.)
Where's Junior?

SUSANNAH: That's right. You've been gone for a few days. Or has it been a week? I lose track.

BOBBY: Where's my son?

SUSANNAH: Over to Daddy.

BOBBY: I warned you.

*(*BOBBY *grabs* SUSANNAH*'s arm. She yelps. He tightens his grip.)*

SUSANNAH: Let go, Bobby. Enoch!! I'm still your wife.
(She shakes herself loose.)

BOBBY: Did anyone see?

SUSANNAH: Does anyone see you? How could anyone see all the way out here?

*(*BOBBY*'s glare scares* SUSANNAH.*)*

SUSANNAH: It wasn't my fault.

BOBBY: Then whose fault is it?

SUSANNAH: I've been being good. You'd know that if—

BOBBY: We cannot afford to lose stock.

SUSANNAH: You gave her to me. She was mine, to do with as I pleased. It's not like the buck.

BOBBY: You're making us pariahs.

SUSANNAH: That will pass. People soon forget.

BOBBY: Dan Henry won't go to the tavern with me anymore. People point and stare.

SUSANNAH: What about James? Surely you have one friend left in the world. With all your righteousness, you make for excellent company.

(BOBBY *shakes his head in disgust.)*

SUSANNAH: I should be more important to you than anything. Not what they think. What you think is more important to me than anything else in the whole world.

BOBBY: Where's her body?

SUSANNAH: In the alfalfa field.

(BOBBY *grabs a shovel.)*

SUSANNAH: Once I started, I couldn't stop. A raging came over me. I could only let it flow through me. When I caught hold of myself, it was too late.

BOBBY: You continually defy me.

SUSANNAH: No.

BOBBY: Yes. You're grown full of spite.

SUSANNAH: That's not it. The midwife believes I'm with child again.

BOBBY: Do I have to be glad?

SUSANNAH: You said this was what you wanted. A full quiver.

BOBBY: In a house filled with peace and human feeling.

SUSANNAH: Is what I've done wrong? Inside myself, I don't feel I'm wrong at all.

BOBBY: How? Can you explain it to me?

(End scene)

Scene 23

*(*BOBBY *enters, sweaty and dirty, with the shovel.* SUSANNAH *now wears a shroud.)*

(She guides one of his hands to the shroud and the other to her belly.)

SUSANNAH: I'm not sorry.

*(*BOBBY *removes his hands.)*

BOBBY: No more.

(He snatches the shroud and rips it.)

(End scene)

Scene 24

*(*BOBBY *sleeps in a chair with his son's baby blanket.)*

*(*SUSANNAH *enters in a night gown and robe. She shakes him. He jumps. A flicker of disgust)*

SUSANNAH: You're afraid to be in our bed.

BOBBY: Don't be foolish. I got up to check on junior. He was unsettled.

SUSANNAH: Because of me.

BOBBY: He feels that something's wrong. I decided to lay with him. It got late so I stayed.

SUSANNAH: You didn't want to wake me.

BOBBY: Mothers need their rest.

SUSANNAH: What about wives? Or is your only care for Junior now?

BOBBY: When we became parents, Junior became the focus. He and what you're now carrying.

SUSANNAH: I still hunger for you.

BOBBY: That's indecent.

SUSANNAH: You never thought so before. You didn't stay for a second. Again. You came in, turned around, and walked right out.

BOBBY: You were pretending to be asleep.

SUSANNAH: To spare both our feelings.

BOBBY: Then that was a lie. Beg god for forgiveness.
(He stands.)

SUSANNAH: There's a lot of blood in our fields. It's never done any harm.

BOBBY: If we're too cruel, they could turn on us and slaughter us in our sleep.

SUSANNAH: They wouldn't dare.

BOBBY: My mistake was trying to teach you by example. I should've sat you down. There's a reason we maim instead of kill. We're not animals. We think and plan. When you maim, it sets a standard.
(He pulls out the calfskin pouch.)
This binds me and my hands. There's no more need for violence between us. It put the fear of god into them and makes them work harder. What you did, took food out of our mouths. No one else. Why would you do that to us?

SUSANNAH: I never…

BOBBY: We try to protect you ladies from having to deal with these realities. But you've crossed over the line too many times.

SUSANNAH: I wish I could make you understand.

BOBBY: If you need to do it, you don't do it yourself. We make another nigger do it.

(SUSANNAH *gasps.)*

BOBBY: I have to talk this way for you to hear me. Do you know how you look when you get your hands dirty for no reason at all? It makes you a mockery to the slaves and the other planters. Shows that you don't have control of yourself.

(Lowers his voice)

Don't ever forget how precarious our position is. It's miles to your father's house and thirteen to town. If they were to revolt, that's a lot of ground to cover.

SUSANNAH: I'm not afraid.

BOBBY: You should be, because I am. I'll pick out another wet nurse. She takes orders only from me. And she'll watch over you.

SUSANNAH: I can't comply with that.

BOBBY: I don't want you alone with our children. Go to our bible. I need you to think on your sins. Perhaps you can still be redeemed.

(SUSANNAH *walks to the Bible stand. She surreptitiously slips one of her grandmother's knives into her pocket.)*

(She reaches the stand, her back to BOBBY.*)*

(BOBBY *silently takes the whip down from the wall.)*

BOBBY: Read Colossians 3, Verse 18.

SUSANNAH: Wives, submit yourselves unto your own husbands, as it is fit in the Lord.

(BOBBY *slowly approaches* SUSANNAH *with the whip.)*

BOBBY: Now Verse 22.

SUSANNAH: Servants, obey in all things your masters according to the flesh; not with eye service, as men pleasers; but in singleness of heart, fearing God. Oh,

Bobby. I've read this a hundred times, but I finally see. She shouldn't be dead, just broken…

*(*SUSANNAH *turns.* BOBBY *gestures for her to turn back.)*

BOBBY: Verse 25.

SUSANNAH: *(Increasing rapidity)* But he that doeth wrong shall receive for the wrong which he hath done: and there is no respect of persons.

*(*BOBBY *raises the whip.)*

*(*SUSANNAH *spins around to confront him with the knife.)*

(Black out)

(End scene)

END OF PLAY

www.ingramcontent.com/pod-product-compliance
Lightning Source LLC
LaVergne TN
LVHW020657100826
845148LV00012B/2540

* 9 7 8 0 8 8 1 4 5 9 0 1 2 *